WORDS WANDER

SHREYA ANIL

To my grandma who lives in my heart for eternity.

To my ammaaaaaa

To my chaaaaaa

To my baby sistah

To God with love...

Contents

Preface

"Hey you !
Why wonder when words wander
and touch the filthy flesh
or the misty mind
or the savage soul
or the sacred benevolence.
Whatever it may touch
it has the vigour to metamorphose
anything from savage to saintly
from filthy to purity
from being misty to precise
words can alter any mind
That's how words wander around
In quest of thee."

- Shreya

Acknowledgements

My deepest gratitude to mom Ragini for supporting in my endeavours.

My thanks to Notionpress for publishing my book.

1. Flames

In your face
they act
in your absence
they talk.
It's hard to perceive
that people who loved
were actually vicious
and merely fake.
They're like flames
that you will love in distance
but once close
they will teach you pain.

2. In the Dead of the Night

I ran into the woods
with a lantern in my hand
In the dead of the night
searching for someone.
Searching for a girl
who got lost in the dark
but nothing new in that
coz she was always, lost.
The night couldn't get any darker
and so couldn't her heart
the night was getting colder
and so was her thoughts.
She ran into the woods
with a lantern in her hand
in the dead of the night
searching for herself.

3. Motherhood

*The ten painful months
with all those sacrifices
her favourite clothes doesn't fit
she can't have her favourite food.
She walks so hard
holding her back
dragging her feet
struggling , of jeez !
She can't cough
she can't sneeze
her bladder can't hold
she feels numb.
She loves a soul
that she haven't met
it's the purest love
one you can't describe.
She gave birth to a life
sacrificing her time
just hoping that
her baby will love her twice
as much as she loves her child.*

4. In Her Happiest Times

I sit on the sea shore
with my legs crossed
counting the waves
and my eyes hugging the blue sky.
The salty breeze
makes my tangled hair fly
I looked up in the air
and gave a blissful smile.
Wondering about the future me
who would be laying on a couch
too tired to keep her legs crossed
she'd be smiling with teary eyes.
Looking at that old polaroid picture
she took in her happiest times
remembering all those days
that made her happy like a baby who smiles.

5. The Words

When you want to blurt out
but you hesitate to do so
your eyes , they speak a lot
coz the words,
the words are
confined under your breath.

6. Her Ethereal Beauty

The sparkle in her eyes
the way her hair flies
the grace in her smile
makes them gaze for a while.
Her dark ebony skin
and her soul without sin
her mind with the depth of an ocean
and her stare like an entire constellation.
Her anger a raging tempest
born to tame the dragons
her curvaceous sway
makes them forget their way.
Her ethereal beauty
was made to embellish the world!

7. The Girl Behind Her

A girl behind her
with lots of worries
living life in a hurry
happy with nobody
still laughs with many.
Good in faking smiles
with a mind shaking inside
who cries in the rain
so nobody could see
whose favourite colour was yellow
but now black.
Who looks like a lily
but a dead red rose
the one with fiery eyes
and a mind like starry skies
who knows if the girl behind her
is broken deep inside.

8. The Rich Heart Under a Poor Coat

Too thin , too fat
too tall , too short
too dark , too fair
you cant wear that , you have many scars!
World went psychotic
by making others lunatic
what happened to this lively world
humanity has perished.
Judging a book by its cover
they admonish people by their size
they believe it's all about the looks
criticizing others without realizing
they too , have flaws.
People are not oblivious
that it's not about the size
not about the scars
not about the skin
and not about the garb.
and when they ask,
"Then what is it about ?"

don't be dread
to broach your voice
and let the world know
that its all about
the rich heart under a poor coat.

9. Till Death Do Us Part

Let's not make promises
that can't be kept
coz promises are often broken
according to the roads taken .
It's not about the vows we make
it's about what we do
no matter if we talk or not
let's always be in each other's heart
no matter how distant we are
be it miles apart
let us hold the strenght in our love
till death do us part.

10. The Voice in my Head

Oh voice in my head
don't yell don't screech
don't whisper
don't repeat.
Oh voice in my head
I can hear , I can perceive
oh voice in my head
you work so hard
harder than my heart.
Don't puzzle things up
and intensify my thoughts
the anxiety you give
burns me alive
I wish for your absence
so that I can revive.
The words you persist
are hard to resist
oh voice in my head
I wish you were dead.

11. Solitary Sea

You and me
we are two different streams
that meets
in a solitary sea.

12. Made of Fire

They thought they could destroy her
but they were unaware
that she was made of fire
because it was transpire.
Life taught her
hurt raised her
she went through a lot
hell than you'll ever know.
She was not born strong
she was made strong
fierce like flames , rage untamed
can't ever be chained.

13. Why Should I Change ?

When she laughs
they call her a psycopath
when she cries
they say she is going through a lot
when she is quiet
they say she's depressed
now she doesn't know what to do
she is so lost daydreaming .
She'll be in her world
all day long
wishing no one comes
and label her as wrong
no one really helps
even her shadow leaves when she yells.
No one had the time
to hear all her weeps
she sat alone for long
and thought about it all
and asked herself why?
Why she should change?

People are so wrong
coz they got no good jobs
when they , themselves ain't happy
they'll go make others the same
she realized she shouldn't change
so she started to smile great
coz she knows
anyways they'll just hate !

14. Staring at the Stars

She sits near the window
staring at the stars
in the middle of the night
with her lurid desires.
She feels forlorn
with no one to appraise her
No matter the divine
things she does
she always gets ignored.
Though she knows
everyone's unconcerned
she sits near the window
staring at the stars
with her eyes filled with tears
tears filled with hope.

15. Refashioning the History

Oh the bell rang,

its time to learn the lies.

Its time to learn about the dead.

Yes! Its the History period.

Even the teacher got bored

teaching things no one knows.

Who knows if its true?

Who believes afterall?

Teaching about the dead

who shed their blood

for nothing but just

to make trouble for us.

Since I couldn't sleep

in between class

as my conscience

worked Alas!

All I could do

was to draw shades on Napoleon

and chain for Hitler

and I sat refashioning the History.

The End For A New Beginning.

• 19 •

www.ingramcontent.com/pod-product-compliance
Lightning Source LLC
Chambersburg PA
CBHW021158130726
47988CB00004B/1669